Plate Tectonics

Sunny Daze

BookLeaf Publishing

India | USA | UK

Presentation by *BookLeaf Publishing*

Web: www.bookleafpub.com

E-mail: info@bookleafpub.com

ISBN: 9789363310629

First edition 2024

These poems are dedicated to all of our Dreamers: our Elders, our Mothers, Fathers, Brothers, Sisters, Our Lovers between the Binary, The Children of our Future and the People in the Present.

My Dog Willow, and the Women in my Life who have supported me through the darkest nights.

It is because of you, that I recognize my light.

Leap Towards a Dream

My Dear,
How your feet will follow your heart most
surely
On days when most relieved
Of fear and absolutes.
Beyond logistics and all doubts.

My Dear, how your feet will follow your heart
Most cautiously
When the path seems dark and winding.
When the lanterns have gone cold and
you've forgotten your name way back home
alone.

Oh, my Dear,
how your feet will follow each other,
Left, right, left,
marching on and on through the night,
through the dimly pale moonlight,
wandering through the thickest trees,
trying to find the dock...

Oh, my dear,
how your legs begin to tremble,
With the weight of uncertainty of step,

Left, right, left,
down a plank thinning and splintered,
What lie below- a mystery.
Dark waters and a strong current out towards the
sea.
With eyes closed and heavily,
caught breathing and sinking-

You pray for one last miracle,
Of what may befell you upon The Leap.

Do you trust your feet?
To guide you through the woods,
To hold your anxious body still and steadily?
Do you trust your heart to beat each morning?

Do you know it will all come to an end?
The Bliss and the Pain,
The Moon, Sun and the Rain.

and to come to trust,
that you will never know, what you have never
known,
and what you've come to know, knows you,
as you stare our across the water-
into the vast deep blue,
wandering through the time that you wont catch
up,

-You follow your feet
and you choose to take the Leap,
without knowing what lies beneath,
and you will trust yourself to swim.

You will trust yourself to swim.

Full Speed Ahead

I thought about writing a poem
Once
About those last precious moments of light,
Right before the sun goes down on the waning
day.

I thought about writing a poem
Once
About all those moments that would just go on
forever and ever and
How every day these days just seem like;
Days gone by-
Just memories
Just poems
like Broken Hearts;

Just poems about those poems you wrote about
those moments-
Before trying to find your way back home in the
dark
Again,
Still holding on to those last few seconds of
light,
And how
They never last forever like you want them to.

Remember when you would play with the
flickering light as a child,
You said,
"It burns in the best ways during those summer
days-
Hot and Bright like the sun.
And I love the way her rays turn everything
golden-
Like the days when my parents still loved each
other and my brother was still alive."

You want to hold them close with the sun's
warmth in your fingers forever-
and whisper-
"Things are totally going to be okay someday,
aren't they?"

so,
I thought I'd finally write a poem
About all of those small moments and all of the
big ones in between,
The sun and it's setting on our long spun golden
summer days,
that we'd stretch out forever on end-
-Numbered and counting-
Until one day, we die again.

Full fast.

Full speed.
A Full day of hard work and of love and family.
A poem about today
Yesterday and Tomorrow's new beginnings.

Piano Man's Lover

Will you play your piano for me?
In the pouring, relentless rain-
When the electricity goes out-
in the house-
In the candle light-
While the world continues to crash down
Around our feet.

In the chaos of the setting sun and
When the days that never seem To never come,
finally have dawned;
Will you keep playing for me?

I hear the glass shattering loudly,
I feel the heat of the sun fading away from my
face.
I hear the way your fingers are beginning to
forget,
How to play songs you've burned into your
fingertips-
In the pouring, relentless rain-
When the electricity goes out-
in the house-
In the candle light-
While the world keeps crashing down

Around our feet.
Will you play for me?
even when you've forgotten the harmony?

Paradise Lost

This poem was written in High Hopes;
to encompass all the Magic
From all those deep places in Lovers hearts-
Where the only true expression of these depths
Is the expansion of their experience together,
Laying next to each other
under the stars fixed up in the heavens,
fingers interlaced- and wondering,
About the ever complex and complicatedly
beautiful,
Unwaveringly eruptive,
Passionate moments engulfed in hot Bliss
unmatched even by:
Rolling Orgasms and Dark chocolate licked off
of a Sunday night.
Red Wine, Warm Summertime.
The kind of Magic we've seemed to have
forgotten.

What have we done when we've forgotten how
to love,
To have forgotten how to fall so hard
we forget we're even falling in the first place.
Weightless and flailing

With much less grace than the creation it took to
create us.
Yeah, that kind of Magic.

This poem was written in High Hopes;
To be unlike any other;
Translated through the angels
Of your long forgotten salvation-
Deeper than the wells your tears well up from.

do you think those same angels would still be
Singing and singing the praises of your name,
When,
All the while-
Her Headlights have been blinding you-
Dizzy and disoriented,
Displacing your projections
Your ego altered reflections,
Mirrored back into your eyes-
The truest sung Radiances of your divine and
human ignorance,
Magic in a dark Disguise.

The unmistakable death dance we were all born
knowing,
and have never fully have forgotten.

May this Poem may help you to remember;
That very moment you looked into her eyes-

On That same disorientating day you went
running
in the pouring downfall of red rain
When,
you asked her to dance in it with you one last
time.

That in very moment, when you would both
forgot your own names-
And Dissolved into each other,
Like an effervescent and glittering spring,
flowing on and on forever
downstream,
Slowly and surely,
soaking in the ever present magic of:

Love and Love Lost and of Lost Lovers in
Paradise.
Just like you and me, used to be.

My Love

My love,
oh, my love,
how long these lessons have shaped me
My Love
oh, my love,
you were never meant to be convenient,
nor were you created to be confined,
limited or defined.
My love,
oh, my love,
you were not taught to operate
under the assumption of risks.
Until you were.

My Love,
you cannot be found between my legs
Maybe you can not even be found within my
heart.
Are you in the air?
Are you Everywhere?
Do you smell like roses or rain?
-like tears or like champagne??

My Love-
there is no need to be jealous,

And in your Abundance, over zealous
Can you surround me Forever,
and pour down around me
like the Rain my soul's been has been aching for
For Decades,
quenching a thirst I've lived with since a child-
My Love,
thank you for helping me to learn,
that I can finally Let it all Go-
Of the fear to weather the Winter alone,
Without a warm place to rest my weary bones,
Light the Fire, dear one,
There is no Place like Home.

My Love,
you are here,
Together and with me-
Rising like the burning sun
Never setting on the Darkest Days
And you Will Burn
on and on and on,
My Love
you have Hurt me
you have hurt them,
And all the others who've tried to Love me
before
you could.
I am so sorry.
And,

I am not,
My Love
Would we have more Poetic Potential,
If we could just learn how all of this is supposed
to work?
One Day-
or two at a time.
Today,
I have Chosen my place in line.
right at the font,
and always on time
My Love,
you are Safe in this heart of mine.
Safe in the hands of other's hearts,
however gentle they chose to hold you.

My love, you are my responsibility.
and I will tend to you tenderly,
so that you are so Safe to bloom,
in an world so often shrouded in gloom
I am safe in you, my Love and you in me.

Ms. Smith's Lucky Poem # 6

Your sweet eyelashes brushed against my ear.

From behind-you held me tight

Slumped your full weight into mine-
And

We began to softly cry.

As we exhaled the rest of our gifted breath-
Melting us into a being that was:
One Whole.
(Both Together and Apart)

We closed our eyes,
Lost Track of time-

As we drifted away from all of those
Moments and spaces that have held us close all
these years.

Forgetting our names-
We laid there in bliss-
Pure magic, Forehead Kiss

We laid so still,
Shimmeringly and Shrill
We remembered to keep on breathing.

We;
Kept bathing in the magic of this friendship-
Kept bathing in our full goddess glory-
Milk Baths in the Moonlight-
Without even trying at all,
somedays we were effortless-
Others, tenacious.

We kept our eyes closed,
as we drowned in all the Shared and Sacred
tears-

We filled our lungs with the Divine Laughter of:
Children Playing on a Sunny day, Orange Juice
in Hand.

And in that very moment,
We remembered:
This is sisterhood unbounded,
 un-bordered,

With nowhere to run except upwards towards
that hot, beaming Summer Sun;
With no other place to be, than right here with
you,

and you beside me.

Through the brightest days
And the darkest nights.
You're like that pair of shoes that fits just right.

Ringing in The Ears of Hounds

There are days,
When;
I wake up flashing red and blue,
Blue then red-
Some,
Memories of you and of back then,
of yesterday and of last year
and of all of the days in between,
where nothing at all was as it seems.
Then,
There are different days,
When,
I wake up burning-
Some;
Wonderings of me and all of this here,
now and of tomorrow- next year,
And of how the growing pains still sting so
terribly.

Seeming to stretch my bones-
pulling my skin so tightly between my teeth
that I forget it is a smile,
and why I might be doing so in the first place.

Some days it feels as if nothing is moving at all.
When suddenly each sound rings differently
and you can't quite put your finger on when that
when became now and...how,
Like right Now, right in front of me.
Like I thought that I was growing.

Some days I wake up and think of all of things
that are.
Of every consistency and every change that's
ever been.
Of the rocking and the rolling of my body
through time,
and of my mind in the waves that never cease.
In the bed, on the floor, the shower, the sand.

On occasion when I wake,
it is possible to grasp hold of a simple moment.

Like a sun beam shining through the window
onto a warm spot on the red carpet.
These Moments may not seem particularly
memorable,
yet fundamental enough that they continue to
resurface,
again and again and..
If I am lucky,
they bring with them, a new lesson each
dawning morning.

A short second of appreciation,
Of Peace in the flashing of it all.
Of remembering in the constant states of our
human forgetfulness.

And yet
I beg of myself;
"do not be deceived"
That the depths of this day were not limited in
any other way
by anything other notion than a destiny.
Designed with your happiness in mind.

And you should be grateful.
And you should be hopeful.
And you should be scared.
And most importantly;

to take heed;
to be deeply convicted that only you can hold
your own truth.
Only you can wake to remember to choose it.
Or to wonder
Or to grow
Or to smile
Or to dance
Or to play.

Only you can choose which smile you share.

Only you can write those senseless poems about
not quite that much at all.
yet somehow holds the essence of life so gently
in your palms.
Some tangled up words of a writer who sees the
magic
in all of the art that it is to live,
to be loved, and to be shared by all.

And the Velvet Curtain Falls

There is one single moment where it all
converges.
And only a split second later, before it falls back
apart.
Transforming the field in front of you-
passed by from then, into an entirely different
decision.
Where am I to fall?
Where am I to run from it all-
If all this running ever leads me back to,
is the same mirror I've seemed to shatter
every day since eight Grade.

Dear God. What a play.

Great acts and their endless Intermissions in
between.
Performances. Illusions.
And I want to run through the veil with you.
Through a suffocating red velvet curtain-
out across hot concrete,
bare feet slicing through glass
shattered on the side of the road.
Lead me Through some guarded gates
where there is beauty everlasting-

Out Past the rusted iron gates of Eden.

If for merely a second, I pray,
I could gather it all in.
As much as my heart could hold.
As vast and deep as oceans before their risings
As many rocks as I've laid down
at this border of heaven and hell.

Jesus,
I've been Grieving.
If I were to finally fall as I ran,
with arms as full as they can;
from holding myself up,
could I be there to catch me?
Before I fell beneath the Willow tree-
Fetal Position and Bleeding.
Fetal Position and Breathing.

These branches could not shield me
from the rain nor spare me from this humanly
pain.
For My tears did not stop falling For days upon
years.
Moss growing atop my blistered, wandering
feet.

Unhurried, Yet Sufferingly,
I rejoiced.

In an emptiness that was finally found.
At the base of a great Birch-
Watching as the seasons change before my eyes.

And at that one single moment where it all
converges-
As the great velvet curtain closes.
and a standing ovation roars.

We hear it's finally the first of the Spring.
And in a spilt second again,
The Fall,
When all the applause has come to an end.
The dream is over.
And I've gone back to bed.

Cloud Castles

Together We'd built-
Cloud Castles across the horizon,
Glittering and Imminent
High rising up to Heaven.
beyond.
Weightlessly and with Joy,
we shifted material things from one room to
another-
as more and more of our souls vaporized-
The less and less that we cared,
about the front door and the back door.

Or that The backyard was shrinking
or that our front gate had disappeared.
we did not care.

Our televisions dissolved,
our refrigerators liquidated.
We did not care.

As We floated from room to room,
we made love in the mornings and
fed each other dinner in the late nights.

Prism colored water droplets decorated our faces

as we sung at dusk to the stars.

Those same stars hung much closer to us now,
than they did when we were back on earth.

And,
as we drifted and dreamed in each others arms-
we felt a deep thundering begin.
Like a fathers voice booming us deaf
or a train coming with broken brakes
way too fast down a mountain backroad.

You tried to grab my hand,
but I condensed in your grasp.
then quickly absorbed into your silk shirt.

Tears streamed down my face as the lightning
struck near our bed.
Our cloud castle that stood floating for only 3
Texas sunsets began to rumble.

that's when-
I felt myself disappearing and floating far away
from you.
No longer having the arms to reach out for your
face-
We could not share a final kiss before the winds
swept me away,

I called out loudly,
in the middle of the night through the tempest,
that... "I'll meet you back here someday, on the
other side of the storm."
Please remember,
that We may not be in the same form.
Please just remember,
that it is me who will fall upon your face when it
rains.
It is me who runs the gutters of your hometown
full of fresh water,
It is me who will always remember:
making love with you in the mornings
and feeding each other dinner in the late nights.

That night when all our storming worries turned
to vapor and smoke.
And in the morning,
a clear blue sky above us both
-in different times-
And you couldn't seem to remember a single
thing.

De Segovia

I awoke to cooing doves and
Fleeting dreams of a Spanish fairytale come
true-
Still hungover off last night's kisses and maybe
some Champaign-

I was floating this morning
in that fuzzy, warm space between dreaming and
waking up,
You told me you'd hope we'd never have to-
As I lay here naked and questioning-
if this was all just wishful thinking?

With the sun setting perfectly in your eyes,
we recited poetry on the beach.
Love twinkling as young stars would wonder of
which wish to grant next.
A single ray gleamed off your lips as you
brought them slowly back to mine
in a giant sleeping day,
still so unsure if we were in a dream.

We talked about the color of the sky through the
tree leaves

and the way the city lights reflected off the water
and back to our eyes,
As if we were the only ones anymore to notice
them.
is that why the city shared so many of her
secrets?
if we were the only ones who still listened?

and still,
I could not shake my concern for reality-
that this definitely too good to be true
and
of what might happen when returned back
Home.
to Texas-
some 5,000 miles from this sacred spot
across the great wide Atlantic.
Back across the sea where things *seemed* to
be so Different,
another world completely
and all together the same.

It feels too easy here,
to fall in love.
Maybe that's the point- that-
Maybe these feelings need no overthinking
and That's why they are called feelings not
thoughts?

The next day,
You kissed me in the jazz music
and I could not stop catching your eyes,
they spoke much more than I could hope to
grasp for;
To try and create words which weren't possible
before.

We shared one of those "You just had to be
there" type of moments.
Left Speechless yet Full of Poems.
5 short weeks,
And you were there.
And we left our Mark,
on the sepia streets of Segovia,
beneath the Castles and in front of strangers.

I asked you once if this may be a movie skit,
unwritten and if the movie was ending soon-
as it reeled out and waveringly before our eyes.

I hoped we'd never have to wake up.

Or was it that we would never have to go back to
sleep,

as if sleep could somehow suspend these days
on a thread of gold wound up around our
pinkies.

I'd promise this movie would be one worth
watching.
That actor with the burning red hair and electric
green eyes,

Although it's been many more months than I'd
care to count,
I still try to count the freckles on your face.
Falling as fast that summer was spent,
And without any parachutes or
veils of true reality to slow us
We fell hard
And to this day
the scars on my knees remain from the trip-
From the fall,
Nothing to break it except coming back down,
coming back home.

You told me you wanted to take all of this back
to Texas.
Back to our home and introduce a reality
I'm not sure either of us were ready for.
Back to Texas.
Where it would surely all fall apart.

Moonlight Part II

I found you there in the moonlight,
Right where you told me
That you'd gone to lay to rest

Your arms were folded neatly atop your chest
As if to protect your long-gone beating heart
Your soul stood still and suspended in the air
around me
I breathed in it's mist and imagined you'd come
back to kiss me.
The shadows started growing darker as I began
to choke.
The mist then turned to thick smoke,
and I began to panic.
Suddenly someone started screaming,
It sounded exactly like your voice,
They'd forgotten to tell me,
that I was supposed to run
As fast as I could,
turn back down and around,
if it ever came to this.

And Then again like old piano keys played too
heavy and out of tune
I misjudged the jump

Ankle twisted.
.cracked.
I felt the pain shoot straight down my back
As sharp as the heart break.

then
Suddenly the sun broke through the trees
And in it's midst,
I heard you singing again
The songs we sung back when we were young
Back when we used to bathe in moonlight
Right here where you'd told me
you'd gone to lay to rest.

one and two

Do you remember that *mourning?
When you finally became aware of
all the world outside your window.

All the cars passing
With all the people,
and their pets inside of them.

You probably remember the shrill sounds of the
sirens and chaos wailing.
But also of the birds singing and the gentle rain
upon your face,

Kissing your forehead with the quite sure-ness
of still-ness in the storm.
Our mothers taught us how to fight for air the
day we learned
it would not only be given to us, as birth-rite,
but that it would taken away one day,
when the men are in power in the West.

Do you remember her voice?
Do you remember the morning,

When we woke up together

sleepy eyes blinking and fingertips wandering-
The way the world feels different after a long
night of dreaming,
And a long morning of wondering:

Will the world ever stop spinning?
Is it even spinning at all?
And do you still think,
We have anything to do with it's pull of gravity?

The old world was lost the day she exhaled
That precious last breath.

The old stories that were left behind,
to be lost in translation:
old warriors of peace turned to dust and Ash and
clay.
Her chest became too heavy that fateful last day,
With the harsh weight of the human's war and
sin.
The sadness of our selfishness left her broken
and then-

Her heart stopped.
buried in a case of forgetfulness
Splinters of fallen trees upon her grave,
stuck right up beneath her fingernails

as she clawed to try and see the sun again just
one more time-
To feel it's warmth and it's light on her skin.
What she would give to feel the rain on her face
just one more time.

Now the new world is on fire-
they have no where left to run
we are suffocating
and can not see through the blaze
Mamma,
we are lost,
and crying out to a god who will not listen

The ash fills our lungs to the brim
That final day as we drowned away in our sins.

"Please, my children, do not call out my name,
when you've forgotten how to swim."

Sacral Women

Palms faced open and up
Stretching outwards into the rain
Daggers digging through her gums
And her in her hunger, it begins.
those growling growing pains.
Nails peeling backwards and bleeding
Her hair in thick matts, tied back.
The color, a deep dark black,
Like the dusty soot underneath her feet.

The ancestors once told me, deep in a dreary
dream,
That she's been crying like this
For decades now-
Barefoot still and Wandering,
All these long miles on end.
She sings about the broken glass,
Once encased around her heart.
It's pain, only a memory now.
And of the same Dreamt visions of the sun,
Once again warming Beaches like religions.
Smiling bright white,
Like blood diamonds Bathing in the moonlight-

Ascending now to heaven,

in a golden coach fit for a queen.
Drawn by black stallions,
One for each of her sins.
and then She screams:
"Have you all lost your count like me?"
Now hooded, sat and laughing,
she sings like an old forgotten siren;

"When will they ever learn- Those men;
Of the forest and its trees,
Of the water and its streams,
Of the heart and all its mysteries.
For they still don't feel the pain,
Of her cut palms from crawling,
Faced down and clenching,
Cleansing slowly in the bloody falling rain.
Daggers digging deep into their discipline,
For a women whose lost her way."
For decades now she's been praying,
Prying through the
Broken glass around her heart.
Yet somehow
Her hunger keeps her singing.
And it's tearing them apart.

They've confused it with her crying,
Saying "they've always felt too much"
Those sacral, sacred women,
With black Matts in their hair.

Amarillo by Mourning

There was an evening once
As the sun set over Texas
And you laid your head on my shoulder
And you asked me about love
And you asked me about death
And you asked me about confusion
And you asked me why the rain falls
And I could feel your heart swelling
And I could feel your tears streaming
And I could feel your head clearing
And I could feel your hands reaching out for:

All of the things in life worth living for
All of the things worth asking about
All of the things we break our hearts over
All of the things we pray to heal us
And sometimes we forget how to let the heart
open
And sometimes we forget to hold our loved ones
near
And sometimes we forget that it's all just so
simple
And sometimes we forget how good the rain
feels-
Soaked into our clothes

Bare feet splashing in the spring
Flowers overgrown on the interstate
Rolling hills and Pink sunsets
Unwaveringly running towards a unborn day
With naivety and splendor and what it means to
be young,
lying your head on your best friends shoulder
and crying and questioning all of the things you
do not yet understand
about life.
about love
about pain

Why can't we all just be free-
With our wandering, Wondering hearts.

And just then, you rested your hand on my face,
with a knowing softness like a mother-
You just looked at me
and we did not have to say any words at all.

Night Terror on Broadway

It is the morning.
Eyes Open and Blinking.
I took a breath in.
I am breathing.
I am shaking.
As the events of all my dreaming,
Came flooding back in;

Like a scary movie flashing on fast forward
Playing backwards, upside down,
making much less sense-
Feeling much more tense as my mind tries to
unravel the spackled scenery.
Unraveling these desperate questionings
Of:
Who was that person?
Why were they here again?
How did they get back into my house? and-
Why do I keep tripping as I try to run away from
them?
   -as if giving them time to catch back up to me
   -like I didn't really want to get away from
them so badly in the first place.
And
How

The blade they were holding during the chase
seemed so sharp (back then)
But-
I can remember it gleaming so bright in that pale
dim moon light-
Casting shadows that they bounced all through
this hall of mirrors,
Guiding me around like emergency exits
To condemned doors
Creaking and splintered Floorboards
Dancing and Flailing and Screaming

And in that same dream that I was dreaming-
I can remember tasting
- blood in my mouth
- the salt from their sweat and from my tears
Mixed with regret and the sweetest scent of our
sin.

I can even remember when,
I would fall down while running
and they would softly pick me back up
with tender touch and such care-
As I screamed and thrashed that:
I wasn't ready
and I don't know if I ever will be.

For their help.
For these sacrifices.

For bandages on my knees.

For their blade to scratch the surface of my skin
while we made love-
And in my dreams, it bled so much,
And in my waking I could not feel a thing.

And in my dreams the air was so thick.
And in my waking the air was still so thick.
And suddenly, I was choking in my bed in the
morning.
On my words.
On my choices.

I was tripping on my feet, and biting through my
own tongue.

My ankles would only give out
as I tried to walk firmly from that burning hell
house.
I could not see the exits clearly,
with this fog of contradictions clouding and
burning my crying eyes.
Gagging on a truth that I could not chew.

Through Everywhere I searched for escape,
I found only windows to climb back inside
Until this suffocating house of cards
finally collapsed in on top of me.

And suddenly I shuttered.
And suddenly I am awake again- gasping for air
and blood in my mouth.

It is a new morning,
some long spun days appeared to have passed
and-
I can't seem to remember why I'm shaking.
Sweating cold Tangled up in my sheets.

And in my waking I struggled to remember
Why in my dream I had been spinning.
I feel dizzy.
Sore palms from some kind of pounding.
I feel confused.
There is scratch on my neck,
and I feel that that is something left to forget.

I question why I woke up to streams of tears
And fading shadows of some carnival house
filled with all of my fears.
And I shake my head slowly and lay a weary
hand on my chest.
It was just another bad dream, I guess.

An Honored Dedication to my Childhood Demon

I once wrote a poem about you
As you and me fell asleep to all the world
Drifting off to that place you never wanted
To talk about when you woke up.

You've been so tired lately
Gripping me so tightly lately,
Those nights when you'd wake in
Fears of falling forever
Or drowning.
Young girl with your
Cold sweats and your
racing pulse,

Trying to out-run demons who
Only taught you how to swim as a child.

I trace my fingers over the old scars on your
chest.
I still hear the shrapnel rattling around in your
small body,
in your bones and heart.

Skin thin and sharp as razor wire lately,

I've only been cut a few times,
you've learned to hold the pressure, and how to
stay calm.
With band aids thick as dragon skin,

Sometimes you taste the blood
to test if you locked inside your dreams-
you tell me,
not to be afraid-
how, Nothing really phases you anymore.

Hollow, An Echo-
But healing,
As you wake now,
Unconsciously walking
some important place fast and out of breath.
Pacing up and down
that same staircase from the basement to the
attic.
"Where the dark ocean and monsters live"
You'd tell your mom as a small child.

"Mommy,
They never taught me how to swim."

 "They never taught me how to swim, and now,
I can't seem to get away form them."

Aguas Calientes

With softly closed eyes,
The silence of the city
rings up the height of the
mountains surrounding her on all sides.
Deafeningly peaceful from up above and far
enough away she sat to listen
as closely as a symphony's final rehearsal.

The breeze carried smells of meats, flowers,
herbs,
the air is fresh and ancient and dripping with a
sickening history of one culture ripped from one
timeline long ago,
across all the stars and back again into another
in which peace is impossible.

With softly closed eyes,
its easy to forget how hot the sun gets in the dry
season,
Or How easy the mud slides when the ground's
been soaked through.
Or how many light skinned explorers in foreign
language and cloth come to walk upon a forcibly
"shared" and sacred land.
And they drink from the stream.

And Oh how they love the corn here. The fruits.
The silver and the gold.
Did they ever stop to think of the spaces upward
in the mountains from which this water flowed?
Of where its flowing towards?
Of where the river may end and of all of the
animals that will drink and lie upon it's shore.

With eyes softly watching, she wrote to herself;

"To live near a river
Is to be in constant surrender
To all of its moments rushing away from you.
Thunderingly and with all of the upswept
memories and
sharp debris of the mind.
Of the heart,
And its roar, it can deafen
And its roar, it can fade
And its roar, it can remind
Of how simple the rush of life can be,
when we choose to sit on the shore,
instead of monetizing it's current.

To sit near a river is to watch-
To learn how to be still in one place
in one time in one spot for one moment
together with the world as its runs itself for once
with out you.

While it all flows on around you,
without you,
Without hesitation, full force-
In its own time and in a path carved long before
an existence of pride"

And sitting here now
With softly closed eyes-
The weight of a spirit's survival unseen and
discounted flows on by.
The way of a life lived by a boy with no mother,
selling single candies near the market.
A tired mom and her baby.
A hungry dog crossing a busy street.
A blind man with sunken eyes selling cold
churros or
playing a harp for tourist who wont stop to
listen.

We try to reach out to touch,
To play some sort of part in the world.
but a transactional moment becomes a
misinterpretation
For connection in a land that's spilt across
timelines and
cant find the space to heal.

Their gods have been disenfranchised.

Their gold stolen from their dead.
Their streets paved over with Spanish
architecture.

These softly closed eyes feel so heavy,
To truly see the broken heart of a people gasping
for their own mountain air
in the heavy shadows of catholic boots.
Of a catholic god with no remorse.
Of crosses, and gold traded for Mirrors and salt.
Of illusions and deceit that trace back for eras
when this river carried to the sea all of its
secrets.
All of its nourishment.
All of it's legacy build on the backs of happy
souls bound to an unremarkable work order of
death.
How Familiar is this story.

All the while as they truly rejoiced, in the eyes
of the world-
Because what they were building was for one
another.
Because it was for their brother,
Their creator Viracocha
(vee~rah~kow~chuh)
Because what they built then still stands now.

And what they stood for still bridges gaps left
from the cracks of a religion that attempted to
dam their same river.

To feel these smooth stones,
to hear the rushing of the times changing,
To see a country still frozen in history.
And to leave behind more than I take.
I can see it.
And to know that world will move on without
me.
And we will all continue to work and to rejoice
and to suffer together,
and we will all continue to sing and to bleed
together and dance for the worries of the world.

And i will remember the moments when her
eyes fell softly closed,
and of how she wrote another poem about
another part of the world
that she never be able to not call her own.
But for a small instance in time,
could call her home.

to all of my relations, that have ever been.
please accept all of my love.

Hostage as my Body Seemed

My eyes fell softly on the horizon that stretched
out before me.
Wanderingly, They blinked in the water colored
setting sun
as my heart ached deep in my chest.
My heart ached as I watched the light fading
dimmer and dimmer ahead of it.
My heart felt as though it would be dark again
soon
and that these feelings would still linger,-
swirling around, untethered in the moonlight to
come rushing back.

My mind thought a lot of things about a lot of
things.
As minds tend to do.
This chartering happens incessantly and without
any particular voice to carry-
Like a silent movie narrated,
unspoken through a series of generally relatable
circumstances.
with a soft song perhaps,
or static visuals reeling a set of memories-
floating along down a railroad far a way forever.

My mind gives me reasons to think about these
thoughts,
churning on for years
I felt as if there was nothing I could do about
them-
and that they may still stay swirling around,
untethered in the moonlight just the same as last
decade.
Minds just do this; I've reconciled.

Settled that it would always be this way.
That I may never see the dawning day when a
dimming of the sun could bring with it a sense
of silence or peace.
Silly me.

My heart always gave me things to feel.
As hearts so often do-
as my mind told me about these feelings and
these feelings lead my thoughts,
Hostage as my body seemed-
I've swam against this shifting current of
lightness and darkness.
I've at last woken to the morning I've been
praying for:
Where I can take in a breath-
while these divisions have space to sit together,
and watch the sun setting on the horizon.

Maybe the stories will tell that this ache will
never end,
and when the sun is dim,
giving way to a night I never asked for.

I've been swimming upstream.
Hostage as my body seemed.

While the moonlight washed over my face, so
did my tears-
mourning the day that was lost to our darkness
as I laid on my back,
wondering when...
I'd lay back there again,
in the grass, and all alone,
remembering all of the astonishing items my
mind and heart held up to the sun of the passing
day behind me.

Closed eyes, hand on heart.
Shuttering now- Lips apart.
Fingers cold and breath shallow-

Hearing the dissonance ring in my mind and the
way it so badly blocked out the night that
surrounded me.
I slowly gathered courage for what felt like ages,
and finally caught my breath -tightly with my
fingertips.

Barely holding on.. And it held me there.
If only for a only a moment and it drove this
ache deeper down
further into my being,
where it may have a chance of resolve.
when-Just then-
Something in me stood still,
and the violent shuttering in my body sent
shivers like earthquakes to the sea.

My heart began to beat and to beat and to beat
faster through to the top of my chest,
as it warmed my blood and shook awake a
silence in my screaming.
A night I've never asked for, coming to an end.
Then,
When,
My mind went quite for the first time since the
sunset,
and for the first time since meeting you,
I felt as though there was a possibility the
darkness could be my friend too,
and that the moonlight could hold its own place
for the shadows within me that needed rest.
And that rest came,
heavy and hard,
and in waves like the tide crashing in my lungs-
A chaos that would inevitably retreat back into
the creation that is the rising sun-

A brand new day, when the golden light did
shine to bathe
all of pieces of me that needed healing and in the
alchemy of a day burned into night and back into
day,
I've grown too much-
I've seen, and listened.
I've welcomed the darkness back home.

and in It's home, I've found refuge.

The Fallen Angel

The sky has been falling since the day you fell
for her.
Tripping two toes to the water and
Damn, did you wait for it.

Lines on hours for days you'd never see again
Hours on nights spent thinking about tripping
and falling-
another unsure drink and
The tipsy fool afraid to finally jump-

Crash landing on the moon too far away from
you
"And you just... stood there."
"You just fucking, stood there?"

Tripping over the sky again
Holding your breath,
like an old friend on the back roads,
dusty and crying,
Slipping in the mud and reaching out to her
through the darkness,
the forest, and the lakes,
That was the night you swore you would never
swim again,

And your head still spins,

Like you've been screaming at yourself
this whole time, wasting-
half centered days spent dreaming about the
nights you may finally meet her again.
But you never will,
she's moved on without a care in the world,
the weight of her fall from grace was not enough
to sanctify your sin.
and no need to try,
you will never win.

You and Me, Sitting Silently

Then again,
like spring time
Finally coming back around-
It's was just you and
it was just me,
Sitting silently together and knowingly
With all our fond memories of wildflowers and
the soft breeze.

Of Times back when time seemed to slip
through our fingers so fast or would just freeze,
still and so lovingly.
Times back when spring meant these flowers
could bloom again like we've been waiting for
all year.
All year.
And It has been fucking long year,
An unforgivable winter,

We sat Mourning all the mornings when the sun
would shine bright back in my eyes.
Those mornings When you would Stare back
into my eyes.
Those days,
When,

You started sinking,
Started getting confused between the truth and
it's illusions-
Started wondering when and how Spring would
ever come around again.
Or If this god damn winter would ever just...end.

One particular day, however, a long time away
when
Years passed while the dead grass burned and
burned for days spent apart,
Fallen leaves and those cold nights when
the wind would shake our old bones, grip us
tight,
like when We'd held each other's hands for dear
life.

'god don't let the wind take her too'

You held so tight that they turned my knuckles
dark blue and then suddenly,
A single flower bloomed;
Right behind her eyes, behind her deep breath,
And she swore she saw,
(and for the last time),
a field of wildflowers,
singing sonnets to the ripped up blue bonnets
and dandelions left wish less.
Skeletons of Dreams left in ruin,

Courageously staying here, to bloom-
She could wait here, for you too,
If you could only stop for a moment to look and
see;
That this was always just a daydream,
A link lost between you and me, when we were
young.
When we didn't know to have faith in all of the
fun,
or how to have faith in all of this Love.
And So we fell,
Back Into dry soil and left on our own for
planting,
To try and grow roots again, searching for water
in a desert-
Our salvation,
Our sanity
in a world that pours concrete over flower beds,
plowed Through our forest's of lover's carvings
in trees left forgotten
and still selling our seeds back to Farmers.
We. Are. Starving.
To be re-planted,
to sow and to reap our joy.
To live and to die.
To love each other
Till Death do we Part.